ENTERTAINMENT & THE ARTS

ROBERT HULL

FRANKLIN WATTS
NEW YORK • LONDON • SYDNEY

First published in 1999
by Franklin Watts, 96 Leonard Street,
London EC2A 4RH

Franklin Watts Australia
14 Mars Road, Lane Cove
NSW 2066

Series editor: Rachel Cooke
Art Director: Robert Walster
Designer: White Design
Consultant: Dr Anne Millard
Picture research: Susan Mennell
Artwork: Peter Bull Associates

A CIP catalogue record for this book
is available from the British Library.

ISBN 0 7496 3294 1 600552301

Dewey Classification 938

Printed in Dubai U.A.E.

Acknowledgements: Cover images: AKG (tr and tl);
Mary Evans Picture Library (b)

AKG London pp. 4l, 20tr (Delphi Museum/Erich Lessing),
5t, 10t, 11bl, 15t, 26b (Musee du Louvre, Paris/Erich
Lessing), 5b (British Museum, London/Erich Lessing), 6r
(Mykonos Museum), 6l, 20-21 (National Archeological
Museum, Athens), 7l (Musee du Bardo, Tunis/Jean-Louis
Nou), 10b, 11t (Kunsthistorisches Museum/Erich
Lessing), 12-13 (John Hios), 15b (Archeological Museum,
Istanbul/Lessing), 22t (Museo Archeologico, Paestum),
23t, 24b (Musee Vivenel, Compiegne/ Erich Lessing),
28t (Staatl. Antikenslg. & Glyptothek, Munich/Lessing),
18, 20tl, 29t; Ancient Art and Architecture Collection pp.
16, 23b, 24t, 25b; AA Photo Library pp. 2-3, 16-17;
Axiom Photographic Agency p. 27b (James Morris);
British Museum, London pp. 8l (E270), 13r (B509), 20b
(xxxvii-viii); E.T. Archive 7r (Capitoline Museum/Erich
Lessing), 13-14 (British Museum), 27t (Vatican Stanze,
Rome), 29b (Museo Nazionale, Rome); Mary Evans
Picture Library pp. 9t, 12b; Eye Ubiquitous pp. 9b (Mike
Southern), 18-19 (B. Whittingham); Robert Harding pp.
13l (Adam Woolfit), 21t (National Museum, Athens);
Hutchison Library p. 8r; Images Colour Library pp. 4r,
21tr, 25t; Katz Pictures/Mansell Collection p. 26t;
Museum of Classical Archeology, Cambridge p. 22b;
Performing Arts Library pp. 11br (Fritz Curzon), 17 (Clive
Barda); Rex Features pp. 14 (Michael Powell), 19 (James
Kelly); Science Photo Library. p. 28b (Omikron)

CONTENTS

STORIES AND STORYTELLERS

For four hundred years or so from about 800 BC, the people we call the ancient Greeks lived in city-states in Greece itself and in colonies round the Mediterranean Sea. Though they lived far apart, they shared certain things that made them 'Greek'. One of these was their stories.

titanic: The word 'titanic' comes from the Titans, the name of some of the first gods in Greece. They were huge brothers of the Giants.

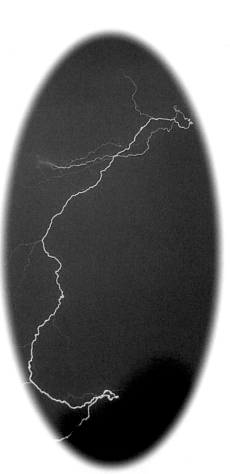

Explaining the world

Like any other people, the ancient Greeks told stories to make sense of their world. These tales called myths explained where human beings came from, how earth, sky and sea were made. They told how the gods, who lived on Mount Olympus, defeated the Giants in a great battle at the beginning of time to gain control over the world.

This sculpture from the Siphnian Treasury in Delphi shows the gods fighting the Giants at the beginning of time.

The Greeks believed that bolts of lightning were the weapons of Zeus, king of the gods.

We still read and enjoy the Greeks' stories. We have all probably heard of Jason and the Argonauts, and the twelve tasks of Heracles, and the monstrous Minotaur in its maze. We might have been told how a great wooden horse was wheeled into Troy, with Greek soldiers hiding inside. After being told and retold – in many different languages – for more than three thousand years, these unforgettable Greek stories are now ours too.

Theseus kills the Minotaur, the half-bull, half-man imprisoned in a maze on the island of Crete.

Heroes

Other stories told how legendary heroes rid the land of monsters or brought new technology to the Greeks; how Heracles killed the many-headed hydra or how Daedalus invented the axe, the drill, and carpenter's glue. None of these stories was written down until after 800 BC. But they were told over and over, from memory, long before: by travelling storytellers, by teachers and by women in the home.

Teaching the Greeks

The Greeks' favourite stories were everywhere. They were told as plays, as written poems, as paintings or sculptures in temples. The stories were not just for fun – they also taught the Greeks about Greekness and how to live their lives. One ruler of Athens organized performances of stories because he 'wanted to teach the citizens, and rule over the best people.'

This 4th-century BC Greek coin shows Heracles, when still a baby, killing two snakes.

HOMER'S EPIC TALES

Two great poem-stories, in particular, filled Greek minds and memories. These were the story of the Greek war against Troy, called *The Iliad*, and that of the hero Odysseus's ten-year journey home, *The Odyssey*. They have become two of the most famous stories in the world.

Today most people believe that there is a factual basis to *The Iliad* and *The Odyssey*, probably events in the dark times of around 1300-1250 BC, when several civilizations seem to have collapsed. In the 19th century, a German archaeologist, Heinrich Schliemann, found Troy with tell-tale signs of burning on ruined walls. He later excavated Mycenae, where the leader of the Greeks, Agamemnon, had come from. He found graves full of treasure, and as at Troy, there were signs of burning and destruction.

This gold death mask was found by Schliemann in a grave at Mycenae.

The Wooden Horse is pulled into Troy. This image was carved on a wine container's neck in the 7th century BC.

The Iliad

The Iliad tells how a prince of Troy, Paris, had stolen Helen, the wife of a Greek king, Menelaus. The Greeks gathered together and sailed to Troy to bring Helen back. After ten years of siege, the Greeks tricked their way into Troy inside their 'gift' of the wooden horse, burnt down the city and set off for home again.

The Odyssey

Many of the Greek soldiers failed to return to Greece. *The Odyssey* tells the story of the wanderings of a Greek king, Odysseus, one of the few who did. The cunning Odysseus had ten years of scares and scrapes, and adventures with giants, monsters and beautiful witches. Finally reaching home on the island of Ithaka, he wasn't even recognized at first. Then he had to throw out of his house the crowd of men who had been pestering his wife, Penelope.

odyssey: We use the word 'odyssey' – from Odysseus – to mean a long, difficult journey. Homer's huge poems are called epics. We call a big, dramatic story an epic adventure – as in the film *Titanic*, for instance.

This 3rd century AD mosaic is Roman. It shows Odysseus tied to a mast to resist the singing of sirens (right).

The poet Homer

The composer of these poems was called Homer. He lived round about 750-700 BC, perhaps on the island of Samos. Homer's story of Troy was woven from many others handed down by story-tellers for hundreds of years. He probably composed it in his head, sometime before 750 BC, though he might have recorded it in writing, and sung it from memory.

Homer, as sculpted many centuries after his death. He is said to have been blind.

7

PERFORMING POETRY

Greeks didn't sit under trees reading poems on their own. Poetry was for performing and listening to with other people. And it was usually sung or chanted from memory. Professional singers – *rhapsodes* – performed *The Iliad* and *The Odyssey* and other stories in this way.

poetry: Many English words about poetry come directly from Greek. 'Poetry' is from *poeio*, meaning to make; in Greece a poet was a maker. 'Rhythm' is from *rhythmos*, meaning an easy flow of sound, or harmony.

A *rhapsode* recites. His first words, not shown here, are 'Once upon a time, in Tiryns...'

An African storyteller today in Sudan. He tells stories passed down by word of mouth over many generations.

Learning by heart

Before there were many books, knowledge had to be kept in people's heads. So Greek school-children learned lots of poetry by heart. 'My father wanted to make me a good man,' one speaker in a discussion says, 'so he made me memorize *The Iliad* and *The Odyssey*.' Both poems all the way through make 27,800 lines of poetry.

Festivals and choruses

Poetry featured in music, dance and in the theatre. Plays were also written in verse and, on important occasions, choruses — groups of about 30 men, boys or girls dressed in costumes — sang poems in honour of gods. Dionysus, god of wine — and drama — had once been turned into a goat for his own protection; his chorus dressed as goats, and sang 'goat-songs'. There were all kinds of choruses, each with its own kind of songs and dances.

The poets Alcaeus and Sappho performing with lyres. Their names are painted on the vase.

■■■ LEGACY ■■■

Writers of today make new translations of Greek poems, and the ancient Greek poems can sound very fresh and modern. This is a recent translation of a simple poem by Sappho written about 2600 years ago. It addressed to the evening star, Hesperus.

> *Hesperus, herdsman of evening,*
> *bringing back home*
> *whatever the light of dawn*
> *scattered: sheep*
> *and goats to the fold,*
> *children to mothers.*

Useful poetry

Poetry was part of everyday Greek life. Greeks often made poems up on the spot, without writing the words down. They had drinking poems, wedding poems, marching-songs, poems to accompany work-tasks or celebrate victorious athletes. Science books and even farming manuals could be written in poetry.

Sappho's poem (above left) might be describing this picture taken in Greece about 2600 years later.

MUSIC EVERYWHERE

Greece was full of music. Men and women sang at the loom, in the forge and in the field, making up tunes and words. At men's dinner parties young women were hired to play the flute, and the diners made up words to sing along.

Hymns and songs

Many other activities involved music and song. For weddings women made up joyous hymns; at funerals they sang laments. And always, story-tellers chanted or sang their tales and accompanied themselves on a stringed instrument plucked with the fingers, perhaps a lyre, or a *kithara*.

This 6th-century BC figurine of a lyre player is 10cm high. It was left at a temple as a dedication.

Sacrifices, festivals, special occasions all needed music. And Greek plays were full of solemn choral dance songs, or comic jigs and tunes. Sports competitions began with music, and there are even vase-paintings of musicians accompanying boxers.

A bull is led to the altar to be sacrificed, while a musician plays a double-flute (an *aulos*).

The importance of music

Music was for everyone to perform, take part in and listen to.
It was a third of the school curriculum – one of the three main subjects. It meant learning to sing and play the lyre and dance. The Greeks believed music trained the feelings, the 'soul', doing for them what gymnastics did for the body.

Different musical instruments were for different occasions. Harsh trumpets, drums and rattles were sounded going into battle; gentle flutes and *kitharae* were for leisure.

A young woman plucks a lute, which had seven strings.

A music teacher encourages his pupil to play with more 'feeling'.

music: 'Music' is from the Greek *mousike* which for the Greeks included literature and the arts, sculpture, poetry, dancing, singing, and so on.

■■■ LEGACY ■■■

We can tell how important music was to the Greeks from their myths and legends. Some of the best-known Greek stories are about music. Modern operas and films have recreated the sad story of Orpheus's visit to the Underworld to find his lost wife, Eurydice. Orpheus was a Greek musician whose beautiful music had the power to attract animals and birds.

Singers from Offenbach's opera *Orpheus in the Underworld*.

DANCING
FOR THE GODS

Greek dancing was often religious. At festivals, choruses danced in honour of a god, telling the story of his or her life in mime and movement, while chanting a hymn.

The dance space, the orchestra, at the theatre of Dionysus in Athens.

Wild dances

Because Apollo was the god of music, dancing for him was probably elegant and controlled. But for some other gods, such as Demeter, goddess of crops and fertility, women dancers might go running off into the countryside and the mountains. But even the wild dances were done in an organized way, on definite dates. The priestesses of Cybele, a nature goddess, performed dances where they pretended to be mad and out of control; they weren't really.

Dancing attendants of Aphrodite, goddess of love. Each deity had their own dance.

Dancing in plays

The choral dance for Dionysus, god of wine, developed into a kind of drama, with actors as well as a chorus. In that way, the chorus became an important part of the Greek play. Choruses might be of human beings, creatures or even things; and a chorus-dancer miming a bird, for instance, or a river, had to learn complicated steps and movements to fit the subject, singing the bird- or river-verses at the same time.

This vase shows members of a chorus in feathered bird costumes.

LEGACY

In modern Greece, dancing is still an important part of festivals. Imagine dancers moving in a ring. In the background a folk-band plays traditional tunes. Sometimes hands are linked with the next dancer's hand. Sometimes hands are in the air, clapping in time, sometimes people turn away, out from the circle then back in. Everyone joins in this modern chain-dance.

Wars and weddings

In Sparta, a city-state where young men had very tough physical training, part of their training was learning different dances. In the Pyrrhic dance, which was also performed in other cities, several men mimed battle-field actions, shooting arrows, throwing javelins and so on — in heavy armour.

In Greece women and men did not usually dance together, but women seem to have danced at home for their own amusement. There was also dancing at weddings, and a chain-dance in which young men and women, holding hands, moved gracefully in a circle.

PLAYS AND PLAYERS

When choruses danced and sang for a god, it was one united choral voice that sang. Then, somehow, the idea developed that another performer, standing apart, could add to what it said, or answer it. Now there were two voices, one the chorus, the other a solitary actor.

A modern chorus performing a Greek tragedy in masks.

This terracotta copy of a Greek mask has a fixed grin. It would have been used in comedy.

drama: Our word 'drama', which we use to describe acting and plays generally, is taken directly from the Greeks who used it in the same way.

The first drama

Perhaps the idea of two voices was first tried by a chorus leader, or a trainer, sometime in the 6th century BC. The experiment caught on. This simple change from one to two voices was the beginning of 'the play' – and all our drama. By the 5th century BC plays were being performed with a chorus and two or three actors. One actor might have several parts, but there were hardly ever more than three actors on stage at once – as well as the chorus.

Comedies and tragedies

Greek audiences saw tragedies, comedies, and rude send-up plays called satyr-plays. Comedies were great fun, with plenty of singing, dancing and rude jokes. The jokes were aimed at things in real life: war, politicians and corrupt juries.

Tragedies were mostly about the grim events of legend, stories that the audience already knew. The Greeks believed that watching these terrible events somehow cleansed them and helped them understand evil.

Two figurines of comic actors in their masks. Perhaps they are sharing a joke.

A woman representing the stage hands a tragic mask to the playwright Euripedes. The god Dionysus looks on.

Putting plays on

Greek actors – who were all male, even for women's parts – were trained professionals, and had to be skilled singers and dancers. They wore masks, sometimes of people the audience recognized.

Masks and other props and clothes cost money, and plays were expensive to put on. There were also writers, musicians, dance-trainers and so on to pay for. All the expense was met by a rich sponsor called a *choregos*. City officials chose him, and men considered it an honourable duty to support the drama.

THE FIRST THEATRES

Greek theatres appeared all over the Greek world, from Sicily to Cyprus. They were open-air, often built against the hillside, with seating in a half-circle.

Earth to stone

The theatre of Dionysus in Athens was probably an earth auditorium until about 330 BC, with the audience sitting on wooden benches.
Late

At the theatre of Dionysus, the god's high priest sat on this throne through every performance.

A day at the theatre

Greek drama was performed at religious festivals in honour of the god Dionysus, god of wine. Starting at daybreak, the audience sat through three or four plays at a time. At the end a jury, chosen from the audience, awarded the writers prizes and a wreath of ivy. There were acting prizes too. The audience was probably nearly all men, although some historians think women attended, too.

A reconstruction of how a later Greek theatre might have looked.

The Greek theatre at Dodona, north-west Greece.
The remains of the *skene* lie behind the orchestra.

■■■LEGACY ■■■

All over the world, in theatres indoors and out, ancient Greek drama is still performed. And the plays have influenced many later writers. Some of the greatest plays of writers like Shakespeare through to Arthur Miller and Eugene O'Neill, have been tragedies, plays based on a Greek invention.

Theatre design

In the theatre, every member of the audience could see, and hear, what went on down on the chorus dance-floor, the orchestra. Theatres had excellent acoustics. At Epidaurus, for instance, from seats high up away from the orchestra, you can hear a dry leaf blowing along its stone floor.

Behind the orchestra was a *skene*, which at first meant a tent or changing room. It later became a solid building, perhaps of two storeys. It was a place 'off-stage' where a murder might take place or actors could appear at windows. In front of the *skene* or at the side of it might be frames for painted scenes. Greek scene-painters were well-known.

A moment of high drama in a tragic play at the theatre today.

17

BUILDERS AND ARCHITECTS

The Greeks were great builders, first in wood and later in stone. Some of their stone buildings still stand 2,500 years after they were built.

A view of the Acropolis, the upper city in Athens. The Parthenon is on its summit.

Planning cities

The Greeks developed great skill in building, using practical knowledge of maths and geometry. They did not just build temples and theatres, but tunnels and harbour walls. Whole cities were planned and built. Early in the 5th century BC the city of Miletus, which an invading Persian army destroyed, was completely recreated with streets in a modern grid-pattern, running at right angles to each other.

This temple of Hephaestus, god of craft, built in Athens in the 5th century BC is very well preserved.

The Parthenon

The Acropolis in Athens seems to sum up the beauty of ancient Greece. Some of the buildings erected in Pericles's time still stand. At the summit is the Parthenon, built for Athena Parthenos, the maiden Athena. The beauty of the building seems mysterious, but what we see is a planned optical illusion. Some 'straight' lines, such as the sides of columns, actually curve slightly. Seen from below, what might have looked heavy seems almost to float.

■■■LEGACY■■■

Athens

Similarly, in 480 BC much of Athens was destroyed by the Persians. Under their ruler Pericles, the Athenians began to rebuild. On the Acropolis, the old high fortress part of Athens, beautiful marble temples appeared. In the centre of the city below, near to or around the market place, there were more temples, housing, council buildings, arcades of cafés and shops, gymnasia, law-courts, and so on.

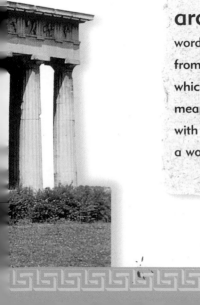

architect: Our word 'architect' comes from the Greek *arkitekton*, which combined *arki* meaning the first or chief, with *tekton*, meaning a worker.

The Capitol buildings in Washington DC were inspired by Greek building – except the dome, which was a Roman invention.

STATUES EVERYWHERE

Greek buildings and spaces were crowded with sculptures of humans, gods and monsters. For St Paul, visiting in the 1st century AD, Athens was still 'a forest of images'.

This 7th-century BC smiling face was carved before sculptors tried to make their work life-like.

'The Charioteer'. This 5th-century BC statue was found at the sacred site of Delphi.

Stone images

These stone images populated streets and buildings, on corners, at entrances, high up against walls or carved from them. High-up ones were sometimes hard to make out, especially inside temples.

High up on the Parthenon, horses gallop along, part of a procession in honour of Athena.

Often sculptures were arranged to retell well-known stories. At sacred sites like Delphi or Olympia, the gods and the giants fought their beginning-of-time battles again, Theseus and Heracles performed their labours, in stone strip-cartoons.

Sacred statues

Sacred statues of gods were often deep inside a temple. Originally they were offerings or dedications, usually of wood. Some of these wooden statues became so sacred they could not be replaced by stone.

But gods would also be pleased by the hard work needed to sculpt stone. Stone was long-lasting as well, and precious. And even if stone was tricky to work because it often split, and then heavy to move, the extra effort and risk honoured the god.

A bronze statue of a god, either Zeus or Poseidon, about to throw a weapon which is now lost.

The Greeks' admiration of the athlete's body is one that we can easily understand. Greek sculpture has been copied and imitated ever since Roman times, and their ideas of physical beauty still influence ours today.

The goddess Athena carved in marble.

Looking alive

As time went on sculptures became less like static monuments and more like athletes in motion. Sculptors carved rippling muscles and flowing clothes, aiming to be realistic. The statues were not left as bare stone but painted bright life-like colours. Some sculptures were even chained to the floor — in case they walked away!

In about the 6th century BC bronze-workers found ways of making hollow sculptures. Bronze sculptures quickly became popular. Postures that couldn't be done in stone were possible in bronze and several copies could be produced from the same mould.

21

PAINTED WALLS AND VASES

The Greek temples and statues we now see in books, or for real, are the colour of their stone. In the 5th century BC they were not; they looked totally different. The Greeks saw brilliantly painted temples and sculptures.

A 5th-century BC painting on the tomb of a diver.

Real-life colours

Traces of faded colour have been found high up on temples; the same kind of residue tells us that the lips, eyes and hair of marble sculptures were coloured in reds, blues, browns and blacks. Marble flesh was sometimes painted with a pale wash, to reduce glare in the sun. And sculptured clothes had bright patterns. All that rich colour has gone.

A reconstructed and painted statue of a young woman, complete with parasol.

22

Wall paintings

Paintings crowded the walls of Greek buildings. Most of them have gone now, but visitors still wrote about them five hundred years after they were painted. They may have disappeared because they were not done direct on the wall, but on wooden frames pegged to it.

We know from writers what some famous paintings were about, and even their size. A painting called *Troy Defeated*, by Polygnotus, in a building at the sacred site of Delphi, was about 16 metres long! His stirring paintings were so popular he was voted free food and lodging for life.

Later vases had more real-looking everyday scenes, like this 5th-century BC vase of women picking fruit.

This 7th-century BC vase features a mixture of animals and geometric patterns.

Painted vases

Though so much has disappeared, we can still see many paintings of ancient Greeks on their vases. First the vase painters did lots of creatures like octopuses, then many geometrical patterns. Later still came gods, athletes, musicians, revellers at parties, plays at the theatre, craftsmen, scenes of women weaving and spinning and collecting water. As the techniques for producing the vases changed, the vase painters made their images more realistic. Their pictures make a large collection of 'stills', which enable us to see the everyday Greek world in action.

SPORT AND GAMES

Greek athletic sports seem to be like ours in many ways. But Greek men had a special reason for being keen on games and fitness: war.

LEGACY

The stadium where we compete or watch is another legacy we have from the Greeks. Their stadium was about 180 metres long, with a starting line at each end, and a turning post, but it was quite narrow. Starting-lines had grooves for athletes' feet, and some probably had a starting-gate, with a wire-release that sprung every pen open at once. The stadium shown here is at Delphi.

'Fighting fit'

In their gymnasia each day Greek men trained to keep 'fighting-fit', literally — they had to be physically prepared for war. Sports competitions had events like chariot-racing and races in armour which were really like war-games. Sparta was different, as in most things. Spartans didn't need gymnasia. Their male citizens lived in army-style barracks from the age of seven till they were thirty, and were always kept fit and on war-alert.

Athlete soldiers running a race in armour. It must have been very hot.

Sporting events

A list of Greek sporting events would be similar to ours, with running, rowing, wrestling, throwing the javelin, jumping, and so on. One event, though, we would not recognize was the *pankration*, an all-out punch-up in which nearly everything was allowed, including kicking, though not biting or eye-gouging.

There were other differences: a runner 'jumping the start' could be flogged. Trainers had whips. And there were usually no prizes for second place.

The long-jump was one of the five events in the Greek pentathlon.

Ball-games

Greeks played ball-games of various kinds. Vase pictures and sculptures show children bowling hoops, young women bouncing a ball, a catching game played between pairs of young men with one on the other's shoulders. There are images of players with curved sticks in a game that looks like hockey. But writers don't describe these games, so we don't know even the basic rules.

This hockey-like game was probably played individually rather than in teams.

WRITERS AND THINKERS

The Mycenaean Greeks had their own way of writing, but it was all forgotten during the dark ages around 1000 BC. The Greeks started to write again when they adapted an alphabet from one of their trading partners, the Phoenicians.

A written record

Written records helped trade, but from the late 7th century BC, Greeks started to write down other things which before then they had memorized: laws, poems, stories, speeches for the assembly or the jury-courts and so on. Writing seemed to make it possible to know and understand more.

By the 5th century BC, all male citizens had to learn to read and write.

The invention of history

For the first time, recent history was written down. The writer Herodotus sailed, walked, and rode thousands of kilometres to gather information and stories for his 'History', a book about the struggle between Persia and Greece. He said 'what people have said to me, and what I have heard, that I must write down'.

Another writer, Thucydides, an Athenian, recorded the long war he fought in between Athens and Sparta, which ended in defeat for Athens.

The historian Thucydides

The beginnings of philosophy

Perhaps it was the Greeks' passion for talk and argument that made them so hungry for true knowledge and understanding. This longing to know they called 'love of wisdom' – *philosophia*, giving us our word 'philosophy'.

The famous philosopher Socrates asked questions like 'What is the best kind of government?', 'Can you teach people to be better?'. The answers he and other Greek philosophers, such as Plato, suggested still influence the way people see and discuss 'the meaning of life' today.

In the 16th century AD, Italian artist Raphael celebrated the learning of ancient Greece in his painting *The School of Athens*. Plato and Aristotle stand at its centre.

■■■ LEGACY ■■■

University students learn by discussing and arguing with their teacher.

One very important idea in modern education is really Socrates's invention – his teaching by asking questions. In one example, Socrates proved, by questioning, that a slave boy already understood a difficult part of geometry. In other words, teaching often means helping people to discover what they already know, without realizing its importance. Finding the truth involves communication, and a lot of answering back, not just listening to one person.

SCIENCE AND KNOWLEDGE

Some of the first Greek writers were what we would call scientists. They studied the world of nature – *phuseos* – and were called *phusikoi* (our word 'physicist').

From myth to science

These scientists didn't believe that mythical stories explained the world. For them the world had to be more orderly and make more sense; it had to be a *kosmos*, a word for troops gathered in battle. The sun wasn't the god Helios pulling a chariot, said Anaxagoras; it was a red-hot stone.

Helios pulling his sun chariot. When Anaxagoras questioned this belief, he got in trouble with the Athenian Assembly for teaching anti-religious ideas.

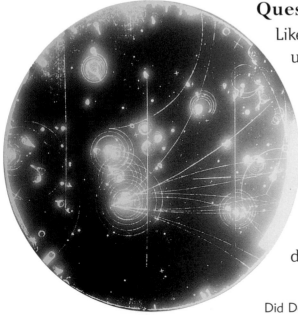

Questions and answers

Like Socrates, these scientists thought the way to understand the world was to ask questions, like 'What is the earth made of?'. Thales, who predicted an eclipse as early as 585 BC, said 'water'; because when you dig you always reach water. Anaximenes said 'air', suggesting stones were air at its most solid.

These early Greek scientists were developing new ideas on astronomy, physics, chemistry and biology. The history of many scientific ideas began with them. Democritus, for instance, invented the word 'atom', to describe the particles that all things are made of.

Did Democritus realize what his ideas might lead to? Now scientists can look inside an atom.

Mathematics

The Greeks also made great advances in mathematics. Some, like Pythagoras, believed the whole natural world could be explained in numbers and sums. His famous theorem about right-angled triangles is just one of many Greek theorems still taught in schools today.

biology: We get our word 'biology', the study of living things, from *bios*, the Greek for life, and *logos* meaning speech.

Pythagoras noted the relationship between volume and sound. His mathematical-musical experiment is recreated in this 15th-century illustration.

The first modern scientist?

In the 4th century BC, Aristotle wrote on many subjects — including politics and poetry. He was fascinated by living things and observed them at first hand. He noted that: 'Flat fish go to sleep in the sand.' He also collected useful information from others: 'Some mariners say they have heard dolphins snoring.'

Aristotle was the first to observe and collect so much information, and organize the things he studied into groups and classes. He invented an approach to studying science that has evolved into the scientific methods we are taught in schools today.

A bust of Aristotle. He was a modest scientist: 'No-one finds out the truth by themselves,' he said.

29

GLOSSARY

acoustics: relating to sound and the sense of hearing. If a room or building has good acoustics, you can hear clearly.

acropolis: the upper part of a city, with a fortress, high about the streets and houses.

Anaxagoras: a Greek philosopher who came to Athens from western Greece in about 480 BC.

Aristotle (384-322 BC): philosopher and scientist who observed and collected information in great detail, then grouped it and used it to develop theories.

assembly: in any city-state, male citizens met in an assembly to argue and decide by voting what laws to pass.

bronze: a metal alloy (blend) of mainly copper with some tin to strengthen it.

chorus: a group of up to 50 singing dancers, often in costume, who sang and performed at festivals. The chorus became an important part of Greek plays.

city-state: a small state that included a city at the centre and the surrounding countryside and villages. From about 800 to 400 BC Greece was divided into a series of city-states, each with their own laws and systems of government.

colony: a settlement of people who have left their own homes to live somewhere else. After about 800 BC Greek cities sent out many colonists, who usually remained citizens of the mother-city.

comedy: a play which aims to be entertaining and funny.

Democritus (c. 460-390 BC): a philosopher from Thrace. He developed the theory of atoms.

gymnasion (plural gymnasia): a Greek sports centre with all kinds of equipment and facilities for 'track and field' events.

Herodotus (c. 480-425 BC): sometimes called the first historian, Herodotus wrote about the wars between the Greeks and Persians.

Homer (c. 8th century BC): the blind poet who composed two great story-poems, *The Iliad* and *The Odyssey*, that were recited and performed in ancient Greece and are still read today.

jury: in law, a group of people who decide at a trial whether someone is innocent or guilty of a crime. In ancient Greece, juries were made up of male citizens, sometimes as many as 501.

orchestra: the dance-floor of the theatre, where the chorus moved and performed.

TIMELINE

c. 1700 BC	Mycenaean civilization emerges.
c. 1200	Mycenaean palaces burnt. Troy destroyed.
c. 1200-800	'Dark Age' in Greece. Knowledge of writing lost.
c. 1100	Greek migrate to coast of Asia (modern Turkey).
c. 1000-750	Phoenicians prosperous, travelling widely.
c 900-750	Geometric paintings on vases.
c. 800-500	Greek colonies set up around Mediterranean and Black Sea.
776	Traditional date for first all-Greece Olympic Games.
c. 750-700	Homer composes his poems.
c. 750	Writing reintroduced to Greece.
c. 725	First stone temple built, to Artemis in Sparta.
c. 700	First human figures appear on vases.
c. 700	Poet Hesiod composing.
c. 650	Free-standing sculptures begin to be made.
c. 600	Sappho living and writing poetry on Lesbos.
600	Temple of Hera built, Olympia.
c. 580	Beginning of Greek philosophy and science.
580	First main temple of Athena in Athens.
534	First Athenian drama festival.

Pericles (c. 495-429 BC): leader of Athens from about 454 to 429.

Persian Empire: the great empire to the east of Greece in Asia, which invaded Greece twice in the early 5th century BC.

Phoenicians: a people from the eastern Mediterranean, who were very successful traders and travellers from about 1050 BC.

Plato (c. 428-348 BC): a leading Greek philosopher, traditionally a pupil of Socrates. Plato's writings and ideas are a foundation of philosophy as it is studied today.

Pythagoras: a philosopher and mathematician who lived in 6th century BC, first on Samos then in Italy. He most famously discovered that when the two shorter sides of a right-angle triangle are squared they add up to the square of the longest side.

Sappho (c. 600 BC): the most famous of several well-known Greek woman poets.

satyr-play: satyrs were countryside spirits, half human and half goat. Satyr-plays were full of slapstick revels that made fun of gods and men alike.

skene: at first, a tent in a theatre where the actors changed. Later it became a solid building, and was used as 'scenery'.

Socrates (c. 470-399 BC): a Greek philosopher whose ideas were very influential in developing Greek thinking and methods of discussion. He wrote nothing down but we know his work through Plato.

Sparta: the chief city-state of the Peloponnese, in southern Greece, and often Athens' rival and enemy. Sparta was famed for its tough attitudes. Its people were constantly prepared and ready for war.

St Paul: the early Christian missionary who travelled round the Mediterranean in 1st century AD teaching the new religion.

theorem: in mathematics, a proof of something that is always true.

Thucydides (c. 455-400 BC): a general in the Athenian army, who wrote a famous history of the war between Athens and Sparta, known as the 'Peloponnesian War'.

tragedy: a serious play in which the central character dies, usually because of some evil they or their ancestors have done. Greek tragic plays were usually based on myth and legend.

vase: a word used to describe Greek pottery in all its many different shapes and sizes.

530	Pythagoras working.
510-490	Great temples built on Sicily.
507	Athens a democracy.
493	Greece invaded by Persia.
487	First comedy performed at Dionysia festival in Athens.
484	Aeschylus wins prize for best play, a tragedy
480	Greeks beaten at Thermopylae by Persians, Athens burnt. Greeks win at Salamis.

479	Greeks win at Platea, Persians go home.
478	'Charioteer' bronze sculpture of Delphi cast.
c. 470	Miletus completely rebuilt after Persian invasion.
c. 454	Pericles leader in Athens.
447	Parthenon begun.
c. 445-426	Herodotus writing.
431-404	War between Athens and Sparta.
431	Thucydides starts writing.

429	Death of Pericles.
428	Plato born.
425	Aristophanes' first anti-war play produced.
404	Athens surrenders to Sparta.
399	Socrates put to death.
387	Plato founds 'Academy' in Athens.
384	Birth of Aristotle.
347	Death of Plato.
335	Aristotle founds a school in Athens.

INDEX